PENGUIN BOOKS
THE BEST OF LAXMAN: VOLUME II

R. K. Laxman was born and educated in Mysore. Soon after he graduated from the University of Mysore, he started drawing cartoons for the *Free Press Journal*, a newspaper in Bombay. Six months later he joined the *Times of India*, a newspaper he has been with, as staff cartoonist, for over forty years. He has written and published numerous short stories, essays and travel articles. Some of these were published in a book, *Idle Hours*. He has also published several collections of his cartoons and two novels.

Mr Laxman was awarded the prestigious Padma Bhushan by the Government of India. The University of Marathwada conferred an honorary Doctor of Literature degree on him. He has won many awards for his cartoons, including Asia's top journalism award, the Ramon Magsaysay Award, in 1984.

R. K. Laxman lives in Bombay.

R. K. Laxman

THE BEST OF LAXMAN
Volume II

PENGUIN BOOKS

Penguin Books India (P) Ltd., 210 Chiranjiv Towers, 43 Nehru Place, New Delhi-110019, India
Penguin Books Ltd., 27 Wrights Lane, London W8 5TZ, UK
Penguin Books USA Inc., 375 Hudson Street, New York, N.Y. 10014, USA
Penguin Books Australia Ltd., Ringwood, Victoria, Australia
Penguin Books Canada Ltd., 10 Alcorn Avenue, Suite 300, Toronto, Ontario M4V 3B2, Canada.
Penguin Books (NZ) Ltd., 182-190 Wairau Road, Auckland 10, New Zealand.

First published by Penguin Books India (P) Ltd. 1993

Copyright © R.K. Laxman 1993

All rights reserved

Typeset in Palatino by Digital Technologies and Printing Solutions, New Delhi

This book is sold subject to the condition that it shall not, by way of trade or otherwise, be lent, hired out, or otherwise circulated without the publisher's prior written consent in any form of binding or cover other than that in which it is published and without a similar condition including this condition being imposed on the subsequent purchaser and without limiting the rights under copyright reserved above, no part of this publication may be reproduced, stored in or introduced into a retrieving system, or transmitted in any form or by any means (electronic, mechanical, photocopying, recording or otherwise), without the prior written permission of both the copyright owner and the above-mentioned publisher of this book.

INTRODUCTION

Mythical characters are not usually the product of their creators' conscious efforts. They evolve over a period of time, shaped and trimmed in the hands of the artists. My Common Man is such a one. He, with his bulbous nose, bristling moustache, bespectacled in check-coat and dhoti is seen day after day caught in battles between chaos and order, greed and power, exploitation and fairplay, bureaucracy and commonsense. He is supposed to symbolize the teeming millions.

When the art of cartooning began to make its stray appearance sometime during the turn of the century, the cartoonist portrayed the common man in any manner he fancied; sometimes as an old-man in rags, sometimes as an emaciated individual and so on, bearing the legend, `The Common Man' on the hem of his clothes.

But when our struggle for independence from imperial domination began to gain momentum, the enslaved masses were symbolized by a sorrow-struck Bharat Mata—a semi-divine being adorning a crown with flowing black tresses wearing a carefully draped saree. The lady did indeed serve the purpose of inspiring patriotism in the heart of the people, inviting them to free themselves from the shackles of British Imperialism.

It would have been awfully anachronistic if I had attempted to prolong her presence in my cartoons to symbolize the common people and their post-independent turmoils. It would have been ridiculous, indeed, if Bharat Mata, for instance, with her crown and untied hair holding our national flag, was seen hanging around in the background, with the bewildered look of my Common Man at a cabinet meeting, or at a glittering state banquet for a visiting foreign dignitary or at the airport to watch a worried minister dash to Delhi or among the pavement dwellers.

Our man now fits effortlessly into any situation and serves the need of representing the people at large. His slight figure and reticent manner are deceptive. He is surprisingly tough and durable and has survived many crises, calamities created by man as well as nature, like corruption, inflation, drought, floods, injustice. In a world which seems to be bent on battering him down he will continue to survive, outliving many politicians and statesmen who profess to lead him to his salvation.

He was already there unnoticed even before the time he walked into my cartoon, where now he visibly resides, playing his omnipotent role as an observer, which he has done for nearly half a century.

27 January 1993   R.K. Laxman

We know you have joined our party. That's not enough. Which group? That's important!

If the population can't be controlled, at least they should make bigger scooters!

No problem. I'll let you have $3 billion, if your situation is that bad. I'll be getting $6 billion from the World Bank, you see.

He is taking a tough stand. He says under no circumstances will he take note of the boycott of the function.

Please, I can't answer your questions because I have not yet become familiar with our national crisis as I was inducted into the cabinet only a few days ago!

... *finally, tomorrow we will take to the street! If that too fails as a last resort we will undertake a protest march from Calcutta to Calicut.*

You are right, 10% cut in perks, salary, travels, transport . . . there is no point in serving the people any more . . . .

As part of the efficiency drive he was prematurely retired, his predecessor was suspended and the new appointee is going to be sacked, sir.

Remind me to tell the High Command that it is impossible to convince these people that the price hike is for their own good!

Where is the cash? Silly boy, didn't you read the morning paper?

Don't be critical. We are dealing with it step by step. First we condemned it. Then we said it shouldn't be tolerated. Then we said it should be crushed. Then . . . .

What I like about him is that he is truly a loyal, disciplined soldier of the party!

Our election defeats are due to infighting, indiscipline, disloyalty, disunity, back-stabbing, etc. And not due to the unpopularity of the Congress.

Yes, we found out why we lost. But we simply can't find out why we won!

Unlike the other projects this has proved the most economical, sir. The loss due to delay in execution has so far been only Rs 12 crores!

You think this is the problem and this is the solution. But I think this is the solution and this is the problem!

No incriminating documents, no cash, no FERA violation! How does the poor man run his business?

No, just wishing that he should become a great Indian is no good! You must pray that he becomes a great non-resident Indian!

Wonderful day at the office. I was not sacked, suspended or prematurely retired today!

... it is intolerable! Something has got to be done! My order that I shouldn't be given so much exposure everyday on the TV, has gone unheeded ....

Since you removed some relatives of yours the department has become terribly understaffed, sir!

Why are you worried? I am not responsible for losing my image and popularity. My advisers are responsible for it.

If you had come a second before, you could have seen him! He came in this way from a tour and left that way on another tour!

It's no use, little fellow. It's not like old times! Pray for the oil price to go up again.

No, the intruders did not take away any cash, jewellery or other valuables. The CBI had taken them away earlier!

Here is a summary of the Commission's 1800-page report, sir— it says we must appoint a commission to examine it and report.

... *at one stage, I gave up all hope and thought I would not escape! But, luckily, I was honourably acquitted ultimately!*

Let's take all the signatures first. When the campaign starts we will use them for or against him depending on the circumstances.

No, it's the other way; the one attacking the Congress rule is the veteran Congressman, and its loyal defender has newly joined from the Opposition.

Between these two blunders we advise you to commit this one, sir. It is easier to explain to the people.

Sorry, no comments! All that I can say is that no action will be taken against me for the muddles and blunders I have been responsible for!

Why, why am I shifted from here to do the party work? I have been loyal, hard-working, efficient . . . .

... the ST bus plunged down here on Thursday! Over there another rolled down on Wednesday! Twenty-five metres away was Tuesday's accident, further up Monday's and ....

Funny fellows! He has just lashed out at them for weakening the party, calling them lazy, selfish and corrupt ... and they are clapping!

Could be a case of slipped disc, sir! . . . they wouldn't have minded really if you hadn't joined them!

Everytime these people come they say they will go back and send us massive wheat aid. What is wheat, father?

No, sir, there's absolutely nothing to report. Everything seems nice and quiet. But you may, if you wish, air-dash to Delhi to be on the safer side.

That chap came and put it on me. Is this the traditional headgear of this region? I have my own doubts.

What will the visitors think if they look at such an alarming picture? Remove it and put a small chart there!

But, in my opinion, this one is clearly a case of language issue and that a case of demand for statehood!

You mean you set fire to the bus without any reason like linguistic, religious boundary? You must be an utterly irresponsible citizen!

Oh, the police caught him! Then he couldn't be a terrorist but an ordinary criminal!

You are so inaccessible, I figured that the only way to see you was to sneak in here in this disguise. I am actually a party member!

Come in, come in! These security fellows have become extremely cautious nowadays and won't let you carry anything in!

The party simply can't waste time like this day after day doing nothing to serve the people—we must consider at least calling a day's total bandh!

I didn't think there's anything political behind this. Maybe it's because they are used to seeing you in the villain's role in all the movies.

They can't find them anywhere! Can you remember where I kept all the incriminating papers? I will be ruined if they are lost!

Don't you believe the press, sir. It always prints sensational lies! Your image hasn't suffered a bit. It remains just as it ever was!

That's a truly honest man! He has kept his sons uneducated and unemployed. He doesn't want to give room for any suspicion that he shows undue favours to his family members.

Supposing they stop making false allegations and start making true ones, what will you do then?

... to counter the misguided move by the Opposition, we will also organize a mammoth rally in support of the unbearable burden of price hike on the Common Man ...!

Your adviser has a point, sir. Such reactions help us to understand if our policy has popular support or not.

I have simplified my work. I read the same speech at all these functions. It has references to human rights, ecology, nuclear bomb, arms race, democracy, science . . . .

You keep bringing problems which have gone out of our hands! Don't we have any crisis which is simple and easy to handle?

Same here; I am very popular outside my country, but inside, my people don't understand me.

I checked with your PRO, sir. He says it will be more popular before this gathering to say that the economy is looking down rather than that it is looking up.

Poor chap. He emigrated to Bombay to beg, but returned because he couldn't find accommodation—on any pavement.

Save the city, save the trees, save the birds, save this, save that. Not a word about saving the people!

OK, we make him the PM! But whom are we to choose as PM after we bring him down? Let's think of that!

Sounds reasonable, sir. He says he can't guarantee a peaceful agitation, but only a semi-peaceful one in which no more than two buses, one private car and three shops will be burnt!

Excellent promises—too good to be wasted on a mere by-election. Let's keep them for the future general elections.

You are a matinee idol, good at sword-fight, gun-play, karate, horse riding, jumping, etc. How come you have not thought of joining the Congress Party?

The minister has warned the centre that if another Rs 168 crores is not sanctioned this project will be doomed!

... *and lastly our plans for economic progress for our state; we will not allow the government to function unless our language is made the official language!*

This problem cannot be solved, as you all know. As for solving the second problem there are many other problems in the way. The next one we are not solving as it will lead to other problems . . . .

When I was close to him he never used to make a single move without consulting me . . . !

That CM was asked to get back and sort out his fight with the rebels himself. It's over a month now. He still hangs around here!

Definitely this is the work of the Congress defectors! Look what they have made our veteran Congress hero do!

The new man has a strange work-style! He comes to the office everyday and attends to the files quietly!

Excuse me, I am the deputy minister in the ministry of what, please?

He is really not so heartless as we thought! He has reduced it from Rs 12 to Rs 7 which was actually Rs 3.

... *and all this apart, my own theory is that if this road digging all over goes on at this furious rate the earth will start to look like this, and soon ... !*

Who?—my PA? Then why didn't you tell me about the steps? You know very well I can't see because my turban covers my eyes!

This serious problem needs immediate attention, sir. You have postponed taking a decision on it for just four months. Would you like to make it six?

What sort of banking system is this? You have already written off the loan you just gave him! You should have allowed at least a week to pass before doing that!

See, even an expert like him is not sure! He started saying it's an extremely good budget and ended up saying it's the worst one!

Is this relief grant for recovering from the ruin caused by this storm or by the previous one some years ago, sir? Then also relief was promised.

Friends, quiet please! It's unreasonable to demand he should extend the fast just because the prices have not come down and disorder continues! He is already too weak . . . !

Trying to be funny? What's the idea crying out, 'tomorrow's news today'!

Here is another instance of police brutality! I have clearly announced that I will self-immolate and they just stand there doing nothing about it . . . .

Yet another building has caught fire! The anti-pollution people are bound to get very, very angry!

You have announced that there has been no quarrel between your colleagues and you! But we investigated and found there has been no such rumour, sir!

I heard him say that he was going to speak out boldly and reveal some very shocking matters shortly. I think he is retiring soon!

I think you should forgive him, sir. He says he had honestly no intention of hurting your feelings when he called you a crazy old buffoon!

Once you have said, 'No comment', why do you have to add that it would damage our image and embarrass the leaders?

I resigned because he wanted me to . . . and I withdrew it because the person over there wanted me to . . . .

We can't ask them to keep off, sir. You did declare that ours was an open government and we wouldn't hide anything from the people.

I'm really sorry for them, you know. When I was living above the poverty line I too used to get terribly upset and worried whenever fares were hiked!

Don't say, '... increase of Rs 20'. Instead write, '... additional surcharge of Rs 20 ....' Put that way the common man won't feel it's a burden.

You may report, 'Interview given on board IAF plane'. Actually I was to have come here by it, it was cancelled at the last minute you know.

I didn't realize the situation was that bad, sir! The cards were distributed as per your order! But they ate them!

No, he has absolutely no criminal record. He has been given the ticket on the basis of his looks, I think.

We will solve this problem within ten days. That's a promise! Give us a couple of weeks to find a solution. Then in a month or two, we will call an all-party meet . . . !

Now the voters have got on to it! Just noticed that except a few in the front row, the rest are all cut-outs!

You will be in trouble for this according to section 42(a) read along with annexure 12A (3) to Ramdas vs State case section III Appendix 7(A) . . . .

I am misquoted! All I meant by it was that you were good, upright and honest and that I would always support you!

This time he has gone too far. But there's nobody to tell him!

I am really ashamed of your incompetence! I asked you to find out and list some achievements of my government and you come and report nearly after a month that you can't find any!

It is agreed then that in the next crisis the breakfast meeting will be at his house, lunch at his, tea and snacks at the one's next to him, dinner at his house . . . .

Why did I leave the Congress? Because I always wanted to leave it ever since I joined it 20 years ago!

No one here at the moment. He was asked to resign. He was asked to be ready for transfer. One there was sacked. That one has gone on . . . .

The High Command says not to yield to the rebels, ignore them and hold on to your seat firmly.

I have plans to improve passenger facilities, of course, like better accommodation, food, bed, breakfast, bath, recreation . . . .

What do you mean fog, bird-hit fuel pump leak, fuse blowout . . . ? I asked what were today's snacks, not snags!

If, implemented, the loss is Rs 250 crores per annum. If it is abandoned, Rs 120 crores per annum. If it is kept pending Rs 40 crores per annum. We will recommend the last option to the ministry.

We are bound to come back to power again! The present rulers are committing the same blunders as we did, and people will throw them out too.

He played a major role as adviser to the last regime, did he? Then thank him, instead of transferring him—he is responsible for your sitting here, really!

Have you done it, sir? Last time you were around, you promised you would table a motion to set up a house committee to examine the drought conditions under the chairmanship of an eminent economist.

No, I won't advise you to promise them water. Promise something simple.

Either way it's a thankless job. You got into trouble for telling a lie! But once I got into a terrible mess for telling the truth!

You don't have to ask for it, sir. Traditionally we vote only for it as we are told it is the only party which will improve our lot!

It has become tight again! I think you have to go on an indefinite fast as a protest against something or the other, once more!

You shouldn't worry about the deficit so much, sir. Millions of our countrymen live with a deficit budget every day of their lives.

I am afraid you can't go on a study tour to understand the needs of those people, sir. Unproductive expenditure has been drastically cut!

It is always the same. Every time we come to complain about the price situation, he himself starts complaining bitterly about it without giving us a chance.

Hard-working man! When he was in power, he worked to improve the lot of his family and friends. Now that he is sacked, he is working to improve the lot of the people.

Today's crisis could be postponed to tomorrow. Postponing the one scheduled for tomorrow to the day after by putting off that crisis to a day following . . . .

You are ruining your future, young man. You had better support it!

We are in a peculiar situation regarding oil. The position is serious but nothing to panic about. It is alarming but not frightening. It is hopeless but not . . . .

I'll tell you why we are returning to our country empty-handed, sir. Instead of asking for the supply of crude oil you went on asking them for edible oil!

Yes, the crowd is pretty thin, but you will find it responsive and intelligent. I knew them well, sir.

You are stealing my idea! I was the first to think of kisans, rural folks, etc. And you are going about talking as if it's your discovery.

Do you believe me at least now that I did not implement all those reforms just to please the masses and win popularity?

The authorities realized that they would never be able to end these digging operations and so constructed the flyovers across the roads!

We must demand still higher wages—prices have shot up since we started the strike!

Yes, that's his new post. It has been created specially for him. But they haven't yet decided what its functions are!

No, we are not taking any disciplinary action against him. He gave a very good explanation for his misbehaviour!

Most of what he is saying isn't true. But I must say it is an excellent criticism of the Centre and a spirited attack on the Congress rule!

It was tough finding a young and experienced person as you wanted, sir. So we had to appoint one young and one experienced!

Oh, I delivered the speech in English, did I? I forgot!

He is bluffing just to get the job. He said he was backward not only socially and economically but also mentally!

Urbanites exploiting rural folks? That's nonsense. My uncle is doing very well in the city. He is a beggar there.

Please don't smile, sir. This picture is to accompany the report on your humiliating dismissal from the ministry.

... *he is honest but has no charisma. This one is good but stupid. The next is disloyal but efficient. He is dishonest, corrupt, unreliable but terribly popular ....*

You said shocking news. Well, where is it?

You thought it was a rumour and issued a denial, did you? But couldn't you see the item projected a clean, flattering image of me?

Sorry, I can't. It would be highly irregular to help you in this matter. If you wish, speak to him. He has a lot of influence over me!
. . . he has improved a lot now. He is rude but not insulting any more.

... *he has improved a lot now. He is rude but not insulting any more.*

He is going on a goodwill mission to Mongolia, Korea and Japan . . . . I thought he at least was honest and clean—but he wants to go via Switzerland!

Technically what he claims is right, sir. He does live within the known sources of his income. It is known to everyone he has Swiss Bank deposits and other hidden investments.

I don't think the discussion is about any project outlay. They are talking in terms of Rs 50 crores and 100 crores! It must be something connected with corruption!

True, you wanted a young man with tact, knowledge and experience. But I couldn't find one like that younger than him.

Amicably settled! Have agreed to 7% reservation of public transport for burning!

Be careful! We will lose credibility if this denying becomes a habit. You said, 'I deny', when that chap said, 'Good Morning'!

It became so frequent, the authorities decided finally to give it a permanent position.

He must have given a very witty reply to those press chaps!

I thought you were a good doctor—so that's what you are up to when we are on strike!

If you chaps are not plotting to overthrow me, then why are you all huddling there and talking in whispers?

. . . *and lastly, let us hope and pray that your fear that the multinationals will take undue advantage of our liberal policy will come true.*

Withered trees, global heat, dried up oceans ... poor chap couldn't bear his own graphic account of the earth in the year AD 8750.

You people are giving lousy programmes perhaps under the impression that nobody is watching. But I am surprised to hear that quite a few still do.

Maybe the cabinet colleagues, well-wishers and admirers have not come to receive you because you asked them not to waste fuel on useless errands!

But all is not lost. No one can beat you as the model for those beautiful 'Crunchy Munchy Vita Biscuits' ads!

Just when do you join our party? You have regularly come for breakfast meet lunch meet and dinner meet for over a month now.

The show-cause notice for indiscipline has been served on every one. Only the peon and the sweeper are left!

Has the economy gone that bad? He took away the coins, maybe, thinking I offered them to him!

It all started with an argument about how to preserve the dignity and honour of the country!

Surely, you are not planning to go beyond the well of the house.

No, I did not faint! It's this bullet-proof vest. Can't they make it a little lighter?

Why did I give up being an industrialist?—because, whatever I did seemed to result in ozone layer damage or afforestation, effluent poison, air pollution, etc.

Just take no notice of it, sir. It is nothing personal. They do this to all politicians from any party!

Poll drive has started picking up, sir. Four dead, fifty injured, ten bomb blasts, thirteen kidnapped ....

I have the High Command's full support. There is absolutely no basis for the rumour that I have resigned! I will know if I have resigned or not only after I go to Delhi!

Of course, I've doubled and trebled the prices! The minister himself has said that price hike is absolutely necessary for growth!

It's a good budget. If we had income we would have enjoyed the relief given to the poor!

Media is simply flocking! He has become big news since he is retiring in the normal course and not been sacked, suspended or asked to go on leave!

He wants a speech written—Pak is aiding the ultras, Kashmir is part of India and no yielding to US bullying—he should have got it all by heart by now!

Tell the mammoth crowd that the protest march against the economic policy is off! We are stuck for a proper slogan!

Oh, the central minister, too! I have a strong suspicion that drought conditions are prevailing in our village!

I have been living here undisturbed for years—thanks to a couple of those boards I picked up somewhere!

Quiet, please! I'll answer any question, at any time, on any subject. After all, ours is a democracy. But under section 23, clause D3, I am not allowed to.

You know, it won't be a bad idea to have a separate ministry to deal with kickbacks, swiss accounts, foreign agencies, etc.

A mammoth crowd, sir. In the announcement I have mentioned that you are a movie star! I hope you don't mind.

Why do you make flattering remarks about the PM every time you speak?—is it bugged?

All that I am asked to tell the press is that the talks were friendly and cordial.

I think when he asked for drinking-water it was for the entire village, sir!

Press, is it? So sorry, there's no news yet. We are still persuading him to withdraw his candidature!

If they are going to let foreign enterprises enter indiscriminately like this, we will be finished!

How have we tackled the economic crisis, your excellency! Well, tighten your belts, ban conspicious consumption, cut wasteful spending, avoid luxury . . . .

I heard father say he might not be able to afford the fee hike and might have to stop my education!

First they wanted a change in the economic structure, then in our taxation method, later in the industrial policy and now they want a change in my style of dress!

By the way, sir, the outlay for it has just been slashed and this project is off. We are holding the function in order not to disappoint the public.

Why have we organized it? —to raise funds to help the poor and the suffering.

This is supposed to be a footpath! . . . of course, Amnesty International won't bother about this sort of thing.

True, the situation is becoming alarming. But, remember it is becoming so under a dully constituted democracy. Therefore, there's no need to panic!

*Excuse me your excellency, how do you pronounce your good name—
Zonctqr sle Bxieyu?*

Excellent new policy, sir. But you must make it vague, confused and complicated, else you will be suspected of acting under foreign pressure!

I assure you there is no such idea. This rumour that we intend to cut down on wasteful expenditure is being spread to create panic among you!

What kind of education are you getting? Did you really think that NRIs are those who responded to the Quit India call?

This is not right, passing this order at the last minute! If I had known about it before, I would have gone round canvassing for votes!

I am from the telephones. Below me the drainage department is digging and below that the water supply department is at work ....

Here is your speech, 'Friends . . . poverty . . . Bofors . . . housing . . . Congress . . . India' . . . it's just about what people can catch as you drive past them making the speech!

Like in all previous elections I have come once more to seek your valuable vote so that I can win and continue to improve your living conditions . . . .

Constable, you are off duty now, aren't you? Then why don't you run and catch the miscreant?

Why is the security so slack, officer? Who is that character standing there?

Disciplinary action will be taken against you if you don't stop that at once! I asked you to order a simple character assassination!

That's all, you just wanted to discuss the State Plan? When your call came I was scared you were going to question me about the awful scandal I am involved in!

... *in simple terms, gentlemen, the polarity of geo-polity causes the ethnic catalytic syndrome counter acting the centripetal forces of universal identity* . . . .

Don't say you won't vote for anyone. You have to. It's highly undemocratic not to vote.

He is visiting the drought areas, is he?

That was a pretty short election speech— 'Whatever my rival promises I'll doubt it'! Obviously you are getting tired!

I warn! If the authorities continue to be adamant I'll be forced to take drastic steps. I will have to ask him to go on an indefinite fast.

We have to travel, meet businessmen, organize trade fairs, arrange seminars to attract foreign capital! This is not enough. We must ask for more!

What do you mean you've done the job? I said, 'Go strip him . . .' and you dashed off before I completed the sentence, '. . . of his party post' I was saying!

Your day's engagements sir; visit to victims of killer brew 8.30 a.m., the fire razed locality 9 a.m., train collision site 9.15 a.m., collapsed bridge 9.20 a.m. . . .

Of course, you can say the prices have come down by 50%, the trade gap has narrowed down to 1/2% and so on. No one will question. This is election campaign!

That's not true! I am always ready to initiate the modalities for proposals to hold tentative talks to motivate moves for negotiations!

These are some excellent charges of corruption. Of course, these are against no one in particular. But we can use them against our colleagues if occasion arises!

We in the government alone cannot bring down the prices. People must agitate, demonstrate, undertake fasts and protest against price rise . . . .

The official report says there is a fall in inflation. So our mass agitation plan against it is working even before we stated it!

Fine time to ask us why we have staged this walk-out! We don't know! We thought you knew!

That's right, sir, only one security guard is on leave. But it is absolutely safe, sir. There are still 424 to escort you!

No more militants left in our custody, sir. We have to arrest a few in order to release them to get our hostages released!

Yes, I have been seeing you demonstrate, shout slogans, go on fast, attempt to self-immolate. But honestly I didn't know it was all to draw my attention!

Don't be silly—not on the floor of the house! He will never be able to do that! He proved his strength on the floor of my office!

If, as he says, he was once a minister holding a high cabinet post, poor man must have been exceptionally honest and incorruptible!

Now he has also joined, sir! The CM has started agitating for his own removal!

Thro' peaceful negotiations? But we have decided to see if we could settle it this way first!

No, I will not resign whatever happens. I have a responsibility towards the nation. But I have every right to threaten to resign!

OK I have emerged stronger from the crisis. But what's the point? My adversary has also emerged stronger from the same crisis.

The trip was useful. By coincidence we both were in New York and we met and discussed Kashmir. Then we ran into each other in Vienna and viewed Punjab with concern. Again in Argentina . . . .

OK, OK, I'll shelve it now! Later, I'll postpone it, review it, have a report prepared and do everything to see I don't implement my new scheme. All right?

I don't want to hear such disrespectful reference, young man. He might say he is just less than a dummy out of sheer modesty. But for us he is a dummy, remember.

We discovered the mystery of this, sir. It was when the nation faced a crisis, all the ministers resigned bringing the administration to a standstill!

We must save petrol. I will walk the rest of the way to the village. You bring the car there later.

What worries me is his utter lack of ambition. He wants to study further, come up in life, serve the nation, etc. But not a word about wanting to go to America!

It is confirmed! The rumour that I am to be appointed the governor of Kashmir is totally false!

He has responded to your show-cause notice . . . . He has shown cause for his anti-party activities and misconduct. They seem quite within our party rules, sir!

Whatever happens don't yield to their pressure tactics! Otherwise our party discipline will be finished!

There he is—you don't come across such truly honest souls these days. He has no foreign bank account, you know!

As an experienced civil servant you should know what action to take—express shock, condemn their behaviour and say you will not tolerate such destruction and violence!

I deny that! I never promised in my election speech I would remove poverty. All I said was I would look into the matter if elected!

That's a good idea! He says instead of clearing them and putting them back every time a VIP comes and goes, why not remove them permanently?

Age of spouse—27!

You may not agree with our decisions, but stop interrupting our discussions and giving your comments. Will you please?

Sort of disciplinary action for his misconduct, I am told! First they took away the portfolio, then the phones, then the table, chair . . . !

... *it is most unfair* ... ! *We are ignored* ... ! *The airport must be named after that great man! Let's find out who he is and make our demand* ... !

I wanted you to see it! Now, where is it? I saw clearly an item which had nothing to do with shooting, killing, bombing, kidnapping, sabotage . . . !

I see problems, worry, changes! I suggest you air-dash to Delhi a couple of times.

Very bad investigative report. It lists eleven allegations of corruption against you but no mention of your vacant land, road transport and building deals!

I am happy that the G-17 Oslo summit was useful . . . . Now, this way, sir, to board the flight to Tasmania for the H-23 summit.

He talks in acronyms and I can't make out! He has asked me to tell SPL that FCL is OK but NDO must give KPT and OHB, excluding NRI a TCBL . . . .

We increased the prices of these items now so that the consumer doesn't feel the burden in the future when they actually go up!

It would be inadvisable to close down this sick unit, sir. Thousands would be out of jobs and there would be trouble.

I am prepared to accept any post and make any sacrifice for the sake of the party, provided I am not disturbed from my present position.

So sorry I used to call you chaps pseudo-Gandhians, fake secularists, etc., If I had known you were all such a nice lot I would have defected long ago!

You repeat that to everyone who comes here! If the food given by the kidnappers was that good, then why don't you go back to them?

Yes, sir, there are awful mistakes of grammar, spelling and syntax. But I did not type it, sir. It came from the World Bank for your signature.

READ MORE IN PENGUIN

In every corner of the world, on every subject under the sun, Penguin represents quality and variety – the very best in publishing today.

For complete information about books available from Penguin – including Puffins, Penguin Classics and Arkana – and how to order them, write to us at the appropriate address below. Please note that for copyright reasons the selection of books varies from country to country.

In India: Please write to *Penguin Books India Pvt Ltd, 706 Eros Apartments, 56 Nehru Place, New Delhi, 110019*

In the United Kingdom: Please write to *Dept. JC, Penguin Books Ltd, FREEPOST, West Drayton, Middlesex, UB7 OBR.*

If you have any difficulty in obtaining a title, please send your order with the correct money, plus ten per cent for postage and packaging, to *PO Box No. 11, West Drayton, Middlesex UB7 OBR*

In the United States: Please write to *Penguin USA Inc., 375 Hudson Street, New York, NY 10014*

In Canada: Please write to *Penguin Books Canada Ltd, 10 Alcorn Avenue, Suite 300, Toronto, Ontario M4V 3B2*

In Australia: Please write to *Penguin Books Australia Ltd, 487 Maroondah Highway, Ringwood, Victoria 3134*

In New Zealand: Please write to *Penguin Books (NZ) Ltd, 182–190 Wairau Road, Private Bag, Takapuna, Auckland 9*

In the Netherlands: Please write to *Penguin Books Netherlands B.V., Keizersgracht 231 NL–1016 DV Amsterdam*

In Germany : Please write to *Penguin Books Deutschland GmbH, Friedrichstrasse 10–12, W–6000 Frankfurt/Main 1*

In Spain: Please write to *Penguin Books S. A.,C. San Bernardo, 117–6° E–28015 Madrid*

In Italy: Please write to *Penguin Italia s.r.l., Via Felice Casati 20, I–20124 Milano*

In France: Please write to *Penguin France S. A., 17 rue Lejeune, F–31000 Toulouse*

In Japan: Please write to *Penguin Books Japan, Ishikiribashi Building, 2-5-4, Suido, Tokyo 112*

In Greece: Please write to *Penguin Hellas Ltd, Dimocritou 3, GR–106 71 Athens*

In South Africa: Please write to *Longman Penguin Southern Africa (Pty) Ltd, Private Bag X08, Bertsham 2013*

FOR THE BEST IN PAPERBACKS, LOOK FOR THE 🐧

THE BEST OF LAXMAN
R.K. Laxman

R.K. Laxman is India's best-known and best-loved cartoonist. For nearly forty years his immortal character, the Common Man, wearing a long checked coat, a dhoti and a perpetually bemused air, has continued to delight and charm readers. This selection, chosen by the cartoonist himself, brings together the best of the Common Man.

'Laughter is our oxygen in these troubled times...and Laxman, through the Common Man, is a dependable source of supply.'
—*Sunday Herald*